Rihanna

Rihanna

MULTI-INDUSTRY MOGUL

HEATHER E. SCHWARTZ

LERNER PUBLICATIONS ◆ MINNEAPOLIS

Read by an expert reader

Lerner Publications Company
An imprint of Lerner Publishing Group, Inc.
241 First Avenue North
Minneapolis, MN 55401 USA

For reading levels and more information, look up this title at www.lernerbooks.com.

Main body text set in Rotis Serif Std 55 Regular. Typeface provided by Adobe Systems.

Designer: Connie Kuhnz

Library of Congress Cataloging-in-Publication Data

Names: Schwartz, Heather E., author.
Title: Rihanna : multi-industry mogul / Heather E. Schwartz.
Description: Minneapolis : Lerner Publications, 2024. | Series: Gateway biographies | Includes
    bibliographical references and index. | Audience: Ages 9–14 | Audience: Grades 7–9 |
    Summary: "Rihanna is an award-winning, worldwide music superstar. But her success
    extends beyond music. She is also a successful businesswoman. Discover more about Rihanna
    from her personal life to her next big projects"– Provided by publisher.
Identifiers: LCCN 2023020210 (print) | LCCN 2023020211 (ebook) | ISBN 9798765610442 (library
    binding) | ISBN 9798765623824 (paperback) | ISBN 9798765614709 (epub)
Subjects: LCSH: Rihanna, 1988– –Juvenile literature. | Singers–Biography–Juvenile literature.
Classification: LCC ML3930.R44 S36 2024 (print) | LCC ML3930.R44 (ebook) | DDC
    782.42164092 [B]–dc23/eng/20230501

LC record available at https://lccn.loc.gov/2023020210
LC ebook record available at https://lccn.loc.gov/2023020211

Manufactured in the United States of America
1-1009629-51717-8/16/2023

TABLE OF CONTENTS

Born in Barbados   8

Finding Fame   13

Surviving and Thriving   15

Taking on New Roles   20

Controlling Her Destiny   23

Fashion Forward   26

Pulling Back from Performance   31

The Life She Created   38

Important Dates   42
Source Notes   44
Selected Bibliography   46
Learn More   47
Index   48

Rihanna performs at the 2023 Super Bowl halftime show.

*O*n February 12, 2023, Rihanna was suspended on a platform high above a crowd of thousands of people. She'd spent hours practicing for her Super Bowl halftime show. She was ready for her first live performance in five years. The audience cheered, and millions at home also watched.

With a determined look on her face, Rihanna lifted the microphone to her lips. She belted out the first song of her thirteen-minute performance. She sang hits from her seventeen-year-long career including, "Umbrella," "Where Have You Been," and "Only Girl (In the World)."

As she sang, Rihanna stood out in a bright red outfit. Her backup dancers wore white. She danced and flew up and down on the platform. At one point, she stopped singing to put on makeup by Fenty Beauty, the cosmetics company she owned. She finished her set with her song "Diamonds." Then she smiled and thanked the crowd. Her performance became the most watched Super Bowl halftime show in history. Rihanna was proud of her performance and what it stood for.

"Representing for immigrants, representing for my country Barbados, representing for Black women everywhere . . . I just think that's really important, [it's] key for people to see the possibilities," she said. "I'm honored to be doing this. . . . It's a beautiful journey that I'm on, and I could have never guessed that I would have made it here."

Born in Barbados

Robyn Rihanna Fenty was born on February 20, 1988, in Saint Michael, Barbados. Her parents are Monica Braithwaite and Ronald Fenty. Braithwaite worked as an accountant and is of Guyanese heritage. Fenty was a warehouse supervisor and Barbadian. Robyn also had three older half siblings: Kandy, Samantha, and Jamie Fenty.

Soon the family grew with the birth of Robyn's younger brothers: Rorrey and Rajad Fenty. Growing up, Robyn loved playing with all her siblings. She was also close with her aunts and uncles. Robyn did well in school, played sports, and was later an army cadet. She also loved music. Some of her favorite artists were Mariah Carey, Celine Dion, and Whitney Houston. She didn't take singing lessons, but she always sang around the neighborhood. She sang so much, people nicknamed her Robyn Red Breast, after the bird called a robin redbreast.

A church in Bridgetown, the capital of Barbados

Ronald Fenty taught Robyn to swim and ride her bike. He also struggled with drug addiction. Addiction is an illness. It happens when a person's brain thinks that they need drugs or alcohol to live. Fenty also physically abused Braithwaite, which made their home unsafe.

Robyn didn't know how to feel about her dad. She had good times with him, but he was also abusing her mother. She felt stressed about the situation. Her grades fell. She stopped spending time with friends. Over time, she didn't talk as much. She was clearly upset. The stress gave her bad headaches. Braithwaite took Robyn to the doctor, who ordered tests to look for a possible brain tumor. "I never expressed how I felt," Robyn said. "I always kept it in. I would go to school . . . you would never know there was something wrong with me."

Discussing Domestic Abuse

Domestic abuse is when someone has a pattern of abuse over another person. There are different types of abuse such as physical, sexual, emotional, and more. Physical abuse includes hitting and kicking. Violence is never okay, and it is not the fault of the person being hurt. The same is true for other forms of abuse.

If you or someone you know is experiencing abuse, you should tell a trusted adult such as a teacher, family member, or school social worker. For domestic abuse, you can call the National Domestic Violence Hotline at (800) 799-7233. You can also chat with them or text them at https://www.thehotline.org/.

When Robyn was around eight years old, her parents separated. They later divorced. Robyn lived with her mom. Her headaches stopped as her homelife grew calmer. Robyn continued to have good and bad times with her dad.

As she grew up, Robyn began expressing herself through music. It helped her release her stress. She didn't have to keep her emotions inside. Robyn continued to sing and express herself.

In 2003, when she was fifteen, Robyn won her high school beauty and talent show by belting out singer Mariah Carey's "Hero." She also formed a girl group with two friends. They sang together during lunchtime at school. The group wasn't serious, but they had fun singing songs by Destiny's Child. Then music producer

Evan Rogers came to Barbados on vacation. One of the girls knew him as a family friend and got the group an audition. They sang together and on their own. Robyn took her shot, singing Beyoncé's "Dangerously in Love." Rogers was blown away. He could see she had star potential. He wanted to sign Robyn as a solo artist.

In her audition, Robyn proved she had raw talent. Still, she was far from ready to record. Rogers wanted to work with her to develop her voice. There was one problem. He lived far away in Stamford, Connecticut. For the next year, Robyn and her mother traveled to Connecticut on school breaks. Then, when Robyn was sixteen, she moved in with Rogers and his wife. From then on, she continued school with a tutor so she could focus on singing. With Rogers's help, she recorded a demo. He also suggested she start going by her middle name, Rihanna.

Rihanna on a TV show in 2005

In 2005 Rihanna recorded her first single, "Pon de Replay." The catchy song combined pop and reggae. Rogers sent the demo to record labels. The first meeting she had with a record label didn't go well.

But then rapper and Def Jam Recordings president Jay-Z called. The Def Jam record label mainly represents hip-hop artists. Jay-Z heard Rihanna's voice and knew he had to meet her.

Rihanna had never met a celebrity. Suddenly, she was being invited to audition for one of the most famous rappers of all time. Arriving at Def Jam with Rogers, she shook with nerves. This was a huge opportunity that could mean the start of her dream career.

When Rihanna met Jay-Z, she was so shy and nervous that she could barely look at him. But it didn't matter. Her voice sounded smooth and clear as she sang a song called "For the Love of You." Then she sang "Pon de

Rihanna and Jay Z attend 2015 Throne Boxing Fight Night at the Theater at Madison Square Garden.

Replay," dancing along to her own choreography. Jay-Z and his team loved her voice. They asked Rogers to cancel Rihanna's meetings with other record labels so they could negotiate. At three in the morning, they reached a deal. Rihanna signed with Def Jam. She was on her way to becoming a professional singer.

Finding Fame

After signing with Def Jam, Rihanna's career began to take off. In May 2005 she released "Pon de Replay" as a single. It soon climbed to No. 2 on the US *Billboard* Hot 100 chart. A few months later, she released her first album, *Music of the Sun.* It had a Caribbean sound, and "Pon de Replay" was its biggest hit. Her second album, *A Girl like Me*, followed in 2006. It sold more than a million copies with two breakout hits, "SOS" and "Unfaithful."

Style Statement

Rihanna wanted to change her look around the release of *Good Girl Gone Bad.* She wanted to cut her hair short, but her record label wanted her to keep her long locks. Rihanna cut her hair anyway. "It made me stand out as an artist," she said. "I don't care who likes it—this is me."

"SOS" was her first song to reach No. 1 on the *Billboard* Hot 100 chart.

Rihanna expressed a new side of herself with her third album, *Good Girl Gone Bad*, released in May 2007. At nineteen, she used the album to express exactly how she felt: rebellious, edgy, and artistic. She collaborated with singers Timbaland and Justin Timberlake on one song. Another song took her career to a whole new level. "Umbrella" was originally written for Britney Spears. But Rihanna recorded it. She gave the song her special style, and fans loved it.

Rihanna performs on the *Today Show* in 2007.

Just two years after leaving Barbados to pursue her dream, Rihanna's singing career was taking off. She stayed true to herself. Rihanna learned a strong work ethic from her mother. She felt a drive to always be doing something to get ahead and follow her dreams. When she wasn't working on songs, she joked around and played pranks on friends.

In 2007 "Umbrella" topped the *Billboard* Hot 100 chart for seven weeks and won awards including two

MTV Video Music Awards. People's love for "Umbrella" kept pouring in. In 2008 Rihanna attended the Grammy Awards. "Umbrella" was nominated for Best Rap/Sung Collaboration. Singer Taylor Swift opened the envelope and revealed the winner. Rihanna and Jay-Z won for "Umbrella."

The two artists took turns giving their speeches. Rihanna joked that she'd promised to give the award to her dad but wasn't sure now that she was holding it. Then she thanked as many people as she could. Everyone she thanked helped her on her musical journey.

Surviving and Thriving

At twenty, Rihanna had success and fame. But it was exhausting to be a star. In May 2008 she decided to make a change. In the future, she wanted more time to rest and reflect.

"In 2007 I didn't really get to enjoy anything that I achieved, because I was moving, moving, moving," she said. "Even at the Grammys, Jay was asking me, 'How does it feel? How does it feel?' I was like, 'When I get home and I lock my room and there's silence, I'll tell you how I feel then.'"

Rihanna and Brown perform at Z100's Jingle Ball in 2008.

Rihanna had a slower schedule until the end of 2008. She still did plenty of performing and touring, but at a more sustainable pace. After the Grammys, she toured for her *Good Girl Gone Bad* album. She also performed at the MTV Video Music Awards, the American Music Awards, and the Z100's Jingle Ball, where she sang with Brown.

Rihanna was nominated for three more Grammy Awards for songs: Best Pop Collaboration with Vocals for "If I Never See Your Face Again," Best Long Form Music Video for "Good Girl Gone Bad Live," and Best Dance Recording for "Disturbia." She was set to sing at the awards. Her life wasn't exactly quiet, but it wasn't as hectic and stressful as it had been in earlier days.

But the night before the Grammys, Brown assaulted Rihanna. The two had a fight that became physical. Brown punched, bit, and choked Rihanna. A witness called 911. Police took pictures of Rihanna's injuries. Brown was arrested and faced criminal charges. The media reported on the event and put out pictures of Rihanna's bruised face. Both Rihanna and Brown canceled their performances at the Grammys and didn't attend the ceremony. Rihanna also canceled her upcoming performances.

People thought that Rihanna had a perfect life because she was famous. But domestic abuse can affect people from all backgrounds. "Before that, I was just a little girl from the island, singing pop music. It was easy to think I was shallow. I had everything. It seemed like I had no problems in the world," she said. "And all of a sudden, one day, boom! Everybody realizes that I do have problems."

Rihanna's relationship with Brown ended the night of the attack. He pleaded guilty to felony assault. He had to do community labor and get domestic violence counseling. He was put on probation for five years.

Rihanna's family and friends supported her. After she began to heal physically and emotionally, she spoke about domestic violence. She wanted people in similar situations to know they didn't have to hide what they were going through and could ask for help.

"I want to give as much insight as I can to young

women, because I feel like I represent a voice that really isn't heard," she said. "Now I can help speak for those women."

Through her voice as a celebrity, Rihanna hoped to make survivors visible. She talked about women, but people of all genders can be victims of domestic violence.

Rihanna also put her feelings into her music as she worked through the difficult situation. She expressed how she was feeling with her new album, *Rated R*, released in November 2009. Her songs were emotional and powerful. She was feeling more in control. She was optimistic about her career and about finding romance in the future.

Rihanna performs during her Last Girl on Earth Tour in 2010.

Rihanna at an event in 2010

Giving Back

From the start of her career, Rihanna worked hard to help others. In 2006 she started the Believe Foundation to support ill children. In 2008 she helped design a fashion line to benefit H&M's Fashion Against AIDS project. AIDS is a life-threatening condition caused by a virus that attacks the immune system.

Some of her charitable work springs from personal connections and experiences. In 2012 she founded the Clara Lionel Foundation, in honor of her grandparents. The organization invests in climate justice in the Caribbean and the US. In 2020 she donated $2.1 million to support domestic violence victims.

Taking on New Roles

In 2010 Rihanna received a new opportunity. Director Peter Berg was casting for his upcoming film *Battleship*. He was impressed with Rihanna's acting on the comedy show *Saturday Night Live*. He had also seen how powerful she was during her concerts and thought she could bring that to the movie. He cast her as Petty Officer Cora "Weps" Raikes.

Rihanna had never acted in a movie before. But she drew on her experience as a military cadet and she was ready to try something new. To get ready for the role, Rihanna trained hard with a real soldier.

Rihanna (*right*) on the *Battleship* poster.

"I had to do tons of push-ups. I had to work out with sandbags that were the weight of the weapons," she said.

The training helped her create the character she was playing. For the film, Rihanna flew to Hawaii and acted on an inflatable raft in the ocean. She did her own stunts, diving into the ocean to rescue swimmers. The filming company had people watching for sharks in the water.

Rihanna and Matt Kemp watch a basketball game in 2010.

Rihanna enjoyed acting. After finishing filming, she flew back to Los Angeles, California, to work on her music. She shot the music video for her song, "Only Girl (In the World)."

For Rihanna, 2010 was a big year. She worked with other artists on her songs "Love the Way You Lie" and "All of the Lights." She was also dating Matt Kemp, a professional baseball player.

At the American Music Awards, she had a bold look with bright red hair. She wore a long, lace dress. People noticed Rihanna's style and were inspired by her looks. After years of performing, she'd become a fashion icon for the ways she played with her appearance.

2010 Grammys

When Rihanna walked the red carpet at the 2010 Grammys, she wore a dramatic floor-length white gown. She won two awards to add to her collection: Best Rap/Sung Collaboration and Best Rap Song for her work on "Run This Town." In his acceptance speech, Jay-Z said Rihanna "made the song everything it is."

Rihanna poses for a photo at the 2010 Grammy Awards.

"Fashion for me is another way I get to express myself creatively. It is one of the fun things I get to do: to play dress-up and create outfits and looks that aren't typical," she said. "I am an artist, so I like creating things."

In November Rihanna released her fifth album, *Loud*. This time, most of her songs were less dark and more fun. She sang about flirting and dating, but she included deeper topics too. Her song "Love the Way You Lie" hit No. 1 on the *Billboard* chart and stayed there for seven weeks. "Only Girl (In the World)" and "What's My Name?" also ranked No. 1.

Controlling Her Destiny

Rihanna had a busy 2011. She was featured on the covers of major magazines such as *British GQ, Vogue*, and *Cosmopolitan*. She talked to *Vanity Fair* about her favorite clothes, beauty products, places to live, and places to visit. She released new videos for songs including "We Found Love." She performed her Loud Tour. In her concerts, she worked the crowd, joining audience members at times and even bringing them onstage.

In June Rihanna partnered with the Barbados Tourism Authority. She promoted her home country to tourists by appearing in advertisements for the island. In August Rihanna brought her tour to Barbados. She performed for twenty-five thousand fans not far from where she grew up and sang for her neighbors. She was so thankful for her country's support and happy to give back to them. Over the next few days, she took some time for herself. She hung out with friends and family. She also relaxed on the water before getting back to work.

In November Rihanna released her sixth album, *Talk That Talk. Rolling Stone* called it "relentlessly catchy and danceable." Her song "We Found Love" with DJ Calvin Harris quickly topped the *Billboard* Hot 100 chart and stayed there for ten weeks.

Rihanna attends a fashion event at the Metropolitan Museum of Art in 2011.

At the Grammys in February 2012, Rihanna gave a powerful performance. She belted out "We Found Love." Next, she joined Coldplay to sing "Princess of

Robyn vs. Rihanna

Throughout her career, Rihanna has projected a strong and powerful public image. But she's a real person with real feelings. She has vulnerable moments too. She created a stage persona to protect herself. She thinks of "Robyn" as her private self and "Rihanna" as her public self.

"Rihanna, that tends to be people's own (creation)," she told *Glamour* magazine. "Robyn is who I am. Rihanna—that's an idea of who I am."

China." In the following months, she performed concerts all over the world.

Rihanna dropped her seventh album, *Unapologetic*, in November. The album had a pop and R&B sound, with elements of other styles like hip-hop and reggae. It was her first No. 1 album on the *Billboard* chart, selling 238,000 copies in its first week.

In 2012 Rihanna and Brown started dating again. Some victims of abuse return to or stay with their abuser. People have many reasons for doing this. Sometimes they might not be able to afford living alone. They might have kids together. It is a complicated choice. After a few months, Rihanna and Brown broke up. This time, the break was final.

Rihanna poses for a photo while filming *Styled to Rock*.

Fashion Forward

Rihanna had plenty of creative projects to keep her mind focused on the positive in 2013. She appeared in A$AP Rocky's music video for his song "Fashion Killa," inspiring him with her style. And she had a cameo appearance playing herself in a movie, starring Michael Cera, Emma Watson, and several more stars. In her scenes, Rihanna had fun acting, singing, and improvising.

Rihanna even got her own reality TV show in 2013. *Styled to Rock* debuted in October with a focus on the singer's passion for fashion. On the series, she selected new, talented designers to compete by creating looks for celebrities including Miley Cyrus, Khloé Kardashian,

Naya Rivera, and Big Sean. She was excited to work with judges including Pharrell Williams, Erin Wasson, and her own stylist, Mel Ottenberg. She also felt good about giving young designers a new and fun opportunity to express themselves. The show ran for one season.

In May 2014 Rihanna left Def Jam Recordings and joined Jay-Z at Roc Nation, the label he'd started in 2008. At Roc Nation, she started her own division, Westbury Road Entertainment. It was named for the area where she grew up in Barbados.

In June Rihanna won the Style Icon Award from the Council of Fashion Designers of America. The award honors a person whose creative style has groundbreaking influence. For the event, she chose a look that was both glamorous and shocking. Her dress was covered with crystals. At the start of her acceptance speech, she said she was nervous and shaking. Then she explained how fashion helped her find her voice and express herself loudly and proudly.

Rihanna delivers her acceptance speech after winning the Style Icon Award in 2014.

Eminem and Rihanna perform onstage at the 2014 MTV Movie Awards.

"I grew up on a really small island and I didn't have a lot of access to fashion. But as far as I can remember, fashion has always been my defense mechanism," she said. "Even as a child, I remember thinking, 'She can beat me, but she cannot beat my outfit.' And to this day, that is how I think about it."

Soon after the event, Rihanna left on the Monster Tour with rapper Eminem. They kicked it off with a sold-out show at the Rose Bowl in Los Angeles. Rihanna was inspired by the rapper. Instead of sticking to her stage persona, she showed more of her real self on the tour.

The following year, she voiced Gratuity "Tip" Tucci in the animated movie *Home*. She joined *The Voice* for the show's ninth season. She collaborated with former Beatle Paul McCartney on the song "FourFiveSeconds." She became fashion brand Dior's first Black spokesperson. Rihanna was excited to represent her culture.

In January 2016 Rihanna released her eighth album, *Anti*. She felt it was her best album yet. The songs felt personal and true to her. "Work" topped the *Billboard* Hot 100 in the US for nine weeks. The album itself became one of the most successful dance albums of all time.

After years of regularly releasing new albums, Rihanna was looking in a different direction. She put her focus on fashion and beauty. Rihanna had always loved makeup. She used it to transform her look, express her mood, and get creative with her style. She was ready to make a business of it. In 2017 she created Fenty Beauty,

Rihanna attends the launch of Fenty Beauty in New York in 2017.

putting her name on her own line of cosmetics. She was excited to work on products so they would be exactly what she wanted. She cared about the textures and colors people would be putting on their skin.

Rihanna made sure that her makeup was accessible to everyone. She made sure the products worked for people of all skin tones, ages, and personalities. It was a lot to take on. But Rihanna had the vision and the work ethic to make it happen.

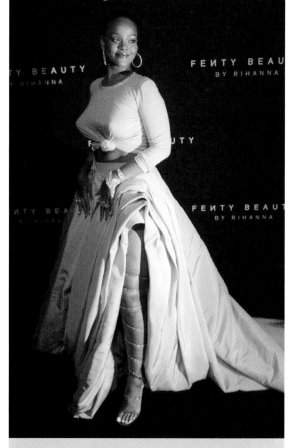

Rihanna attends a Fenty Beauty event in 2017.

By September her products were ready to launch. The launch was during Fashion Week, an event where designers present new fashion collections in New York City. More than three hundred people came to celebrate the start of Fenty Beauty. For Rihanna, the night of the launch felt like both a birthday party and album release.

Pulling Back from Performance

While she developed her beauty brand, Rihanna kept singing. But after performing "Wild Thoughts" at the Grammys in 2018, she put a hold on performances too. Behind the scenes, she was still working on music. But secretly, she feared she couldn't put out another album as good as *Anti*. The pressure was too much. What could she do next instead?

Rihanna performs at the Grammy Awards in 2018.

Rihanna hugs a model during a 2018 fashion show for Savage X Fenty.

In March 2018, Rihanna partnered with TechStyle Fashion Group to launch a clothing line. She had a big goal. She wanted to empower people to wear what they want and own their beauty. Her line offered underwear, pajamas, clothing, and accessories. Rihanna made sure it was accessible with a wide range of sizes and prices. She launched her products in May, calling the brand Savage X Fenty.

Later that year, she launched a special sleepwear collection through Savage X Fenty. Money from the sales went to the Clara Lionel Foundation. Through fashion, she was expressing herself, helping others do the same, and giving back.

In April 2019, a movie costarring Rihanna and musician and actor Donald Glover was released. Rihanna and Glover played a couple living on an island. Glover's character tries to put on a music festival to inspire people. Rihanna loved working on the project.

"It was the greatest experience, being in Cuba, phones off, present with life and art!" she wrote in an Instagram post thanking Glover for the opportunity. "It was humbling!"

Fundraising Fun

In 2019 Rihanna hosted the Diamond Ball, a fancy event in New York City. The event raises money for the Clara Lionel Foundation. The evening included dinner, an auction, and a performance by Rihanna. The event raised $5 million.

Rihanna attends the 2019 Diamond Ball.

Rihanna speaks at a 2017 event for LVMH.

Later that year, Rihanna shared videos on social media that showed she was working on music for her next album, *R9*. But she had also been focused on fashion. Rihanna became the first female celebrity chosen to create a brand for the luxury group LVMH. Rihanna created a luxury fashion company named Fenty for LVMH. Rihanna was excited about her new brand. Fashion let her freely express herself. With music, she felt that she had to do better than the last album. Fashion didn't have that pressure for her.

In October 2019, she released *The Rihanna Book*, a book about her life with more than a thousand photos. Guests packed a museum in New York City for the book's release party. Rihanna spoke to the crowd.

In 2020 the COVID-19 pandemic spread around the world. Businesses and schools closed to stop the spread of the disease. Rihanna wanted to help. She donated more than $5 million to organizations working to feed and treat people during the emergency.

That May, people saw a video of police officers killing George Floyd, a Black man in Minneapolis, Minnesota. People began to protest racism. Racism is the poor treatment of or violence against people because of their race. Rihanna donated to Black Lives Matter, an organization that demands justice for Black people. She also gave money to other groups fighting racism.

The National Association for the Advancement of Colored People gave Rihanna an award for her work. The

Protesters gather in the streets carrying signs to support George Floyd.

Rihanna gives a speech after accepting her award from the National Association for the Advancement of Colored People in 2020.

organization was created when Black people were referred to as colored people. Now the term *colored* is considered to be discriminatory. Rihanna used her speech to point out that racism is everyone's problem.

"We can only fix this world together," she said. "We cannot do it divided."

It was a difficult year, but there were bright spots for Rihanna. She launched a new skin-care line, Fenty Skin.

She appeared on the covers of *Harper's Bazaar* and *British Vogue.* And she released her own *Rihannazine*, a special issue of *i-D* magazine.

Rihanna and A$AP Rocky grew closer throughout 2020 too. They spent the summer on a road trip from Los Angeles to New York. Away from the spotlight, they could relax and be themselves. They grilled food, tie-dyed T-shirts, and just spent time with each other. Rihanna started feeling as though he was family.

In November the pair was spotted on a trip to New York City, visiting a hotel, having dinner with friends,

Rihanna and A$AP Rocky attend the 2019 Fashion Awards.

and taking a walk together. The next month, they let the world know they were dating. For the holidays, they flew to Barbados. They took a sunset cruise on Christmas Eve and celebrated with Rihanna's family.

The Life She Created

In 2021 Rihanna became a billionaire. She was the richest female musician in the world. Most of her money didn't come from music. It came from her fashion and beauty brands. But with eight People's Choice Awards, nine Grammys, and thirteen American Music Awards, she was also a successful musician.

At the end of 2021, she was declared a national hero of Barbados. She was celebrated at a ceremony for her work and accomplishments that honored the island. Many people attended including the Barbados prime minister Mia Mottley, Barbados president Sandra Mason, and Charles, then the Prince of Wales.

"This is a day that I will never, ever forget. It's also a day that I never saw coming," Rihanna said at the ceremony. "I have traveled the world and received several awards and recognitions, but nothing, nothing compares to being recognized in the soil that you grew in."

She kicked off 2022 by donating $15 million toward climate justice through the Clara Lionel Foundation. Later that spring, she became a mother. She and A$AP Rocky had a son. By September, more news was out about

Rihanna is declared a national hero during Barbados's presidential inauguration in 2021.

Rihanna. She was set to headline the 2023 Super Bowl halftime show. Making the commitment was scary. She also had a new baby. But this was something Rihanna really wanted to do.

"When you become a mom, there's something that just happens where you feel like you can take on the world and do anything," she said. "The Super Bowl is one of the biggest stages in the world . . . there's something exhilarating about the challenge of it all."

When the big day came, fans were thrilled to see Rihanna perform. She put on an amazing show. People thought she was showing a baby bump. The next day, Rihanna and A$AP confirmed they were expecting their second son.

Soon after the Super Bowl, Rihanna performed her song "Lift Me Up," from the movie *Black Panther: Wakanda Forever* at the Oscars. While Rihanna had been busy with several businesses, helping others, and being a mother, she never stopped thinking about her fans.

Rihanna performs with dancers at the 2023 Super Bowl.

Throughout her career, Rihanna has shown how much she cares—about music and fashion, about expressing herself, and about making the world a better place.

She puts passion into everything she does. She's worked hard, stayed true to herself, and created more than she ever imagined.

Rihanna performing at the Oscars in 2023

IMPORTANT DATES

1988   Robyn Rihanna Fenty is born on February 20.

2005   She signs with Def Jam Recordings.

She releases her first album, *Music of the Sun*.

2006   She releases her second album, *A Girl like Me*.

She launches the Believe Foundation.

2007   She releases her third album, *Good Girl Gone Bad*.

2008   She wins her first Grammy for her song "Umbrella."

2009   Her fourth album, *Rated R,* drops in November.

2010   She releases *Loud*, her fifth album.

She wins two more Grammys for her vocal work on the song "Run This Town."

2011   Rihanna releases *Talk That Talk*, her sixth album.

2012   Her seventh album, *Unapologetic*, hits No. 1 album on the *Billboard* chart.

         Styled to Rock, Rihanna's reality TV show, premieres.

2014   She wins the Council of Fashion Designers of America's Fashion Icon Award.

2016   She releases *Anti*, her eight album.

2017   Rihanna launches her beauty brand, Fenty Beauty.

2018   She launches her fashion brand, Savage X Fenty.

2021   Rihanna becomes a billionaire.

2023   Rihanna performs at the Super Bowl halftime show.

SOURCE NOTES

8   Mike Bedigan, "Rihanna Says Super Bowl VII Halftime Show Preparations Were Almost Impossible," Wales Online, February 12, 2023, https://www.walesonline.co.uk/lifestyle/showbiz/rihanna-explains-almost-impossible-preparations-26218063.

9   "Rihanna," Biography, updated January 31, 2022, https://www.biography.com/musicians/rihanna.

13   Nicholas Hautman, "Rihanna through the Years: Look Back at Her Rise from Singer to Business Mogul," *Us Weekly*, May 11, 2023, https://www.usmagazine.com/celebrity-news/pictures/rihanna-through-the-years-200919/.

16   Simon Reynolds, "Rihanna Taking It Easy in 2008," Digital Spy, May 8, 2008, https://www.digitalspy.com/music/a95491/rihanna-taking-it-easy-in-2008/.

17   Alex Bilmes, "Red Alert," *GQ*, November 13, 2012, https://www.gq-magazine.co.uk/article/gq-girls-rihanna-interview-photos-only-girl-chris-brown-eminem.

17–18   Laurie Sandell, "Rihanna: Back on Top!," *Glamour*, November 2, 2009, https://www.glamour.com/story/rihanna.

20   "Rihanna Speaks Up about *Battleship* Role," BBC, April 9, 2012, https://www.bbc.com/news/entertainment-arts-17598677.

22   "Jay-Z, Rihanna and Kanye West Win Best Rap/Sung Collaboration at the 52nd GRAMMYs/GRAMMY Rewind," YouTube video, 1:35, posted by the Recording Academy/GRAMMYs, December 4, 2019, https://www.youtube.com/watch?v=iuB_a6J461M.

23   Sandell, "Rihanna: Back on Top!"

24 Jody Rosen, "Talk That Talk," *Rolling Stone*, November 21, 2011, https://www.rollingstone.com/music/music-album-reviews/talk-that-talk-179978/.

25 "Rihanna's *Glamour* November Issue Cover-Shoot," *Glamour,* September 30, 2013, https://www.glamour.com/gallery/rihanna-november-2013-glamour-cover-shoot-gallery.

28 "Rihanna, Style Icon Award—2014 CFDA Fashion Awards Council of Fashion Designers of America," YouTube video, 6:49, posted by the Council of Fashion Designers of America, June 3, 2014, https://www.youtube.com/watch?v=KslXdpe0BCY.

33 "Rihanna Praises Donald Glover, Calls Him 'A True Gem to the Culture,'" YouTube video, 1:19, posted by Billboard News, April 18, 2019, https://www.youtube.com/watch?v=dbubKgCfXC4.

36 Jared Richard," Here's Everything Rihanna Did in 2020 Instead of Releasing Music," Junkee, December 9, 2020, https://junkee.com/rihanna-2020-recap-summary/281280#:~:text=Donated%20More%20Than%20%248%20Million,and%20WHO's%20Solidarity%20Response%20Fund.

38 Dánica Coto, Associated Press, "Rihanna's Officially Titled 'Right Excellent,' Named Barbados National Hero," PBS, November 30, 2021, https://www.pbs.org/newshour/arts/rihannas-officially-titled-right-excellent-named-barbados-hero.

39 Meredith Nardino, "Rihanna's Rare Quotes about Motherhood after Welcoming Son with A$AP Rocky: 'Most Love I've Ever Known,'" *Us Weekly*, updated May 11, 2023, https://www.usmagazine.com/celebrity-moms/pictures/rihannas-best-motherhood-quotes-since-giving-birth/.

SELECTED BIBLIOGRAPHY

Coto, Dánica. "Rihanna's Officially Titled 'Right Excellent,' Named Barbados National Hero." PBS, November 30, 2021. https://www.pbs .org/newshour/arts/rihannas-officially-titled-right-excellent-named -barbados-hero.

"Jay-Z, Rihanna and Kanye West Win Best Rap/Sung Collaboration at the 52nd GRAMMYs/GRAMMY Rewind." YouTube video, 1:35. Posted by the Recording Academy/GRAMMYs, December 4, 2019. https://www.youtube.com/watch?v=iuB_a6J461M.

Nardino, Meredith. "Rihanna's Rare Quotes about Motherhood after Welcoming Son with A$AP Rocky: 'Most Love I've Ever Known.'" *Us Weekly*, March 6, 2023. https://www.usmagazine.com/celebrity-moms/pictures/rihannas-best -motherhood-quotes-since-giving-birth/.

"Rihanna." Biography, January 31, 2022. https://www.biography.com /musicians/rihanna.

"Rihanna." Britannica, March 12, 2023. https://www.britannica.com /biography/Rihanna.

"Rihanna." Recording Academy GRAMMY Awards. Accessed May 20, 2023. https://www.grammy.com/artists/rihanna/5943.

"Rihanna's FULL Apple Music Super Bowl LVII Halftime Show." YouTube video, 13:50. Posted by the NFL, February 12, 2023. https://www.youtube.com/watch?v=HjBo--1n8lI.

"Rihanna Speaks Up about Battleship Role." BBC, April 9, 2012. https:// www.bbc.com/news/entertainment-arts-17598677.

Swertlow, Meg. "A Look Back at Rihanna's Grammy Outfits through the Years." E! News, January 24, 2018. https://www.eonline.com /news/908586/a-look-back-at-rihanna-s-grammy-outfits-through -the-years.

Tietjen, Alexa. "Watch a Teenage Rihanna Belt Out Mariah Carey's 'Hero' at Her High School Talent Show." VH1, April 29, 2015. https://www.vh1.com/news/a108kf/rihanna-sings-mariah-carey-hero-as-a-teenager.

LEARN MORE

Britannica Kids: Barbados
https://kids.britannica.com/kids/article/Barbados/345645

Britannica Kids: Rihanna
https://kids.britannica.com/students/article/Rihanna/570949

Csicsko, David Lee. *Fashion Icons.* Chicago: Trope, 2023.

Elizabeth, Jordannah. *A Child's Introduction to Hip-Hop: The Beats, Rhymes, and Roots of a Musical Revolution.* New York: Black Dog and Leventhal, 2023.

KidsHealth: Abuse: What You Need to Know
https://kidshealth.org/en/teens/family-abuse.html

Kidzworld: Rihanna Fun Facts!
https://www.kidzworld.com/article/26934-rihanna-fun-facts/

Nnachi, Ngeri. *Changemakers in Music: Women Leading the Way.* Minneapolis: Lerner Publications, 2024.

INDEX

"All of the Lights," 21
Anti, 29, 31
A$AP Rocky, 26, 37–38

Barbados, 8, 11, 14, 23, 27, 38
Beyoncé, 11
Big Sean, 27
Braithwaite, Monica, 8–10
Brown, Chris, 15–17, 25

Carey, Mariah, 8, 10
Clara Lionel Foundation, 19, 32–33, 38

Def Jam Recordings, 12–13, 27
Destiny's Child, 10
"Disturbia," 16

Eminem, 28

Fenty, Ronald, 8–10, 15
Fenty Beauty, 29–30
Fenty Skin, 36

Girl like Me, A, 13
Glover, Donald, 33–34

Good Girl Gone Bad, 13–14, 16
Grammy, 15–17, 22, 24, 31, 38

Jay-Z, 12–13, 15, 22, 27

"Lift Me Up," 40
Loud, 23
"Love the Way You Lie," 21, 23

"Only Girl (In the World)," 7, 21, 23

"Pon de Replay," 11–13

Rated R, 18
Rihannazine, 37
R9, 34

"SOS," 13–14

"Umbrella," 7, 14–15

"Where Have You Been," 7
"Wild Thoughts," 31

PHOTO ACKNOWLEDGMENTS

Image credits: Axelle/Bauer-Griffin/FilmMagic/Getty Images, p. 2; MaLija/Shutterstock, p, 3; Kevin Mazur/ Roc Nation/Getty Images, pp. 6, 40; Filip Fuxa/Alamy, p. 9; Michael Loccisano/ FilmMagic/Getty Images, p. 11; Jerritt Clark/WireImage/Getty Images, p. 12; GTCRFOTO/ Alamy, p. 14; Theo Wargo/WireImage for Clear Channel/Getty Images, p. 16; Gie Knaeps/ Getty Images, p. 18; Rob Loud/Getty Images, p. 19; Mary Evans Picture Library Ltd/Alamy, p. 20; Kevork Djansezian/Getty Images, p. 21; GABRIEL BOUYS/AFP/Getty Images, p. 22; Dimitrios Kambouris/FilmMagic/Getty Images, p. 24; Steve Stock/Alamy, p. 26; D Dipasupil/ Getty Images, p. 27; Kevork Djansezian/MTV/Getty Images, p. 28; Kevin Mazur/Getty Images, p. 29; Bryan R. Smith/AFP/Getty Images, p. 30; Theo Wargo/WireImage/Getty Images, p. 31; Kevin Mazur/Savage X Fenty/Getty Images, p. 32; Taylor Hill/WireImage/Getty Images, p. 33; Bertrand Rindoff Petroff/Getty Images, p. 34; Robert Nickelsberg/Getty Images, p. 35; Aaron J. Thornton/BET/Getty Images, p. 36; Jeff Spicer/BFC/Getty Images, p. 37; Randy Brooks/AFP/ Getty Images, p. 39; T. Fallon/AFP/Getty Images, p. 41.

Cover: ANGELA WEISS/AFP/Getty Images; MaLija/Shutterstock.